Sexiest at 50: PTSD PhD Marie

by

Dr. Marie D. Kube, Ph.D. & Dr. Michael G. Klug, Ph.D.

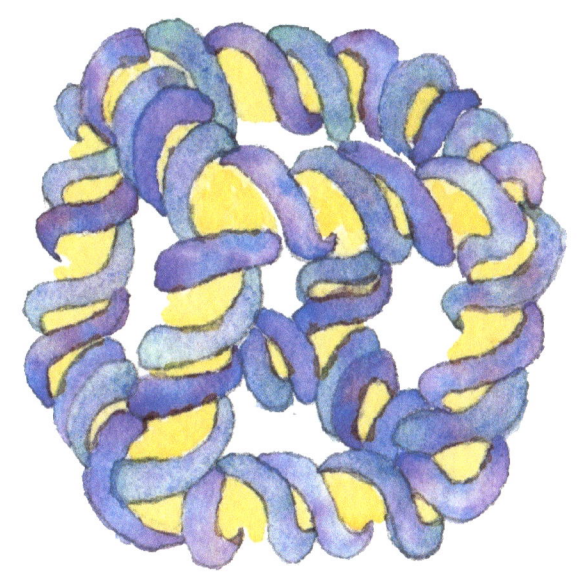

Mary, Mother of Our Lord

Publishing Organization

2038 Ford Parkway #369

St. Paul, MN 55116

Please be heart-healthy to safely enjoy sex and sexy pictures!

Foreword

What if some easy changes to the way you think could change everything in your life? You don't have to change your beliefs to imagine a woman who lost her son to a cruel dictator, a woman whose son was leading the people in a peaceful change to civilization. Her son's advice was not taken, even by those who purport to follow what was said. What would that woman say and do if alive today? What if that woman believed that her child was coming again soon? What would she say and do?

I wish that I could remember and do everything that she ever told me. How many would say that about their ex-wife, mother or sister? As a scientist, I found it impossible that Dagmar, as she was called at that time, could ever be so right. My father-in-law told me at our wedding reception dinner that in order to have a happy marriage, I just needed to say 3 words: "You're right dear."

How many people would say that their spouse was really right and they didn't know that for decades and therefore didn't treat them as they should have been treated? That Marie even talks to me is a miracle, let alone that we are writing this book together. So many more miracles have happened that are undeniable, even as they are unbelievable.

I am an irritatingly skeptical scientist. My wife spent years studying, researching and writing the *Instructions for Helping to Improve the Human Condition*, which you can read at www.myspiritualconnection.org and www.myspiritualassociation.com. Through use of the *Instructions for Helping to Improve the Human Condition*, I am convinced that there is a spiritual side to our existence that is being neglected by most of our current civilization. Knowledge of spirituality and the *Instructions for Helping to Improve the Human Condition* have helped us get through job losses, deaths of parents and family members, and other personal trauma in a very short period of time.

I am doing this to help my ex-wife get to someone way better than me. Most might think that is self-serving. I assure you, however, that I would bring her back and treat her like a queen in the next second, but only if that were the best thing for her. I am arrhythmic while she is a dancer, exemplifying just one of the major cultural barriers that came between us. So, I am doing this to help someone I deeply love to regain her independence from me, facing the possibility of not even seeing or hearing her for some time. Sounds crazy, I know. Yet when I believe in Mary, and the words she speaks as Marie, I am overwhelmed with heavenly bliss. And when I want what I think that I wanted or want, life turns back to hell. I will bet that there are others who feel the same way about Marie.

If we all could choose a heavenly existence for all and actually make that happen simply by making that choice, then how could we not make that happen?

Michael G. Klug, Ph.D.
Twin Cities, Minnesota
July 29, 2017

My Dearest Reader,

Now that I am 50 years old and still sexy, I can tell you that being sexy is not simply a matter of getting dressed up and made up for a photo shoot in some exotic venue. Being sexy is a lifestyle, a way of living. Because I love you so much, I am writing this book to share how I do it with you. All the pictures herein are of me at 50 years of age so that you can see the results for yourself and decide whether to take my advice or not.

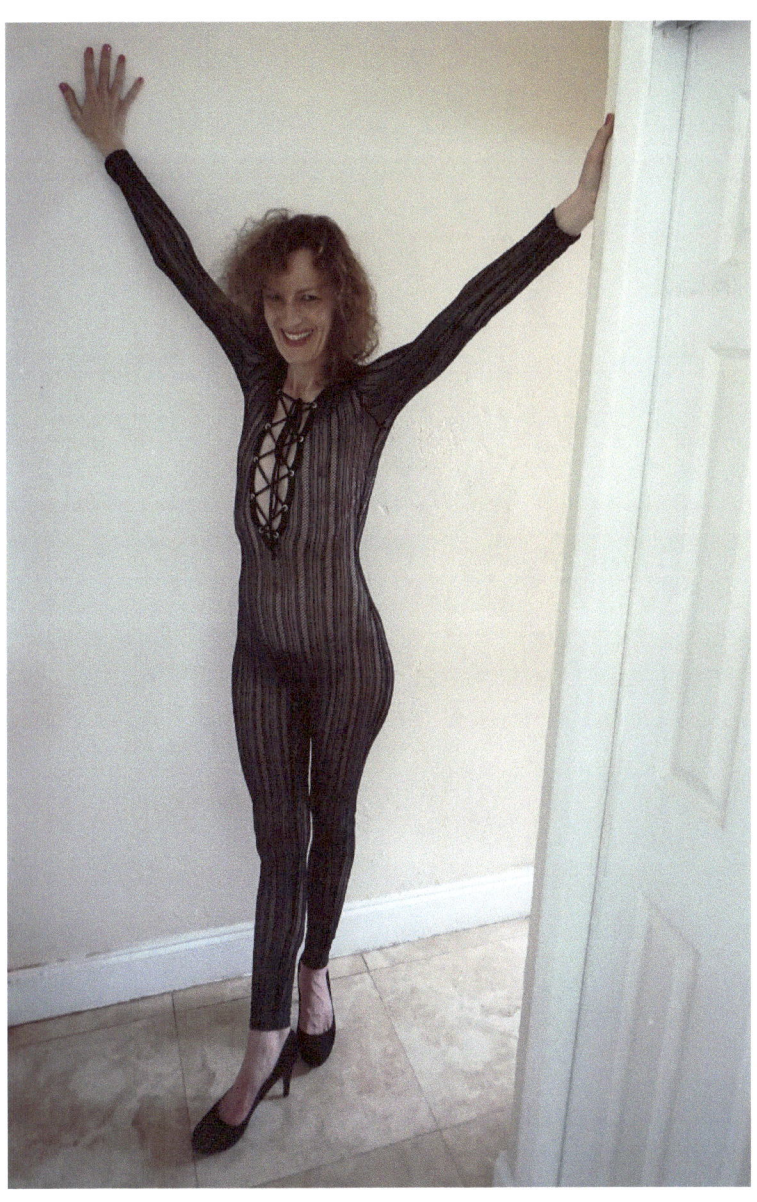

Being sexy means engaging in moderate exercise every day that is low-impact.

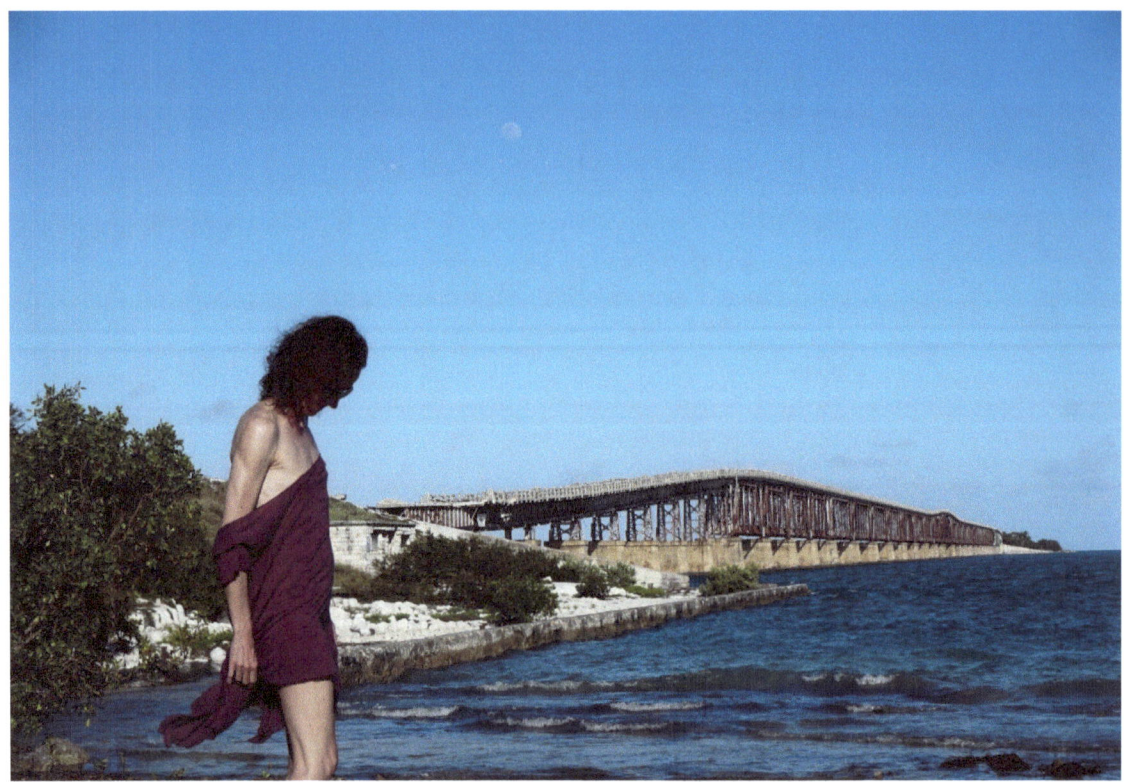

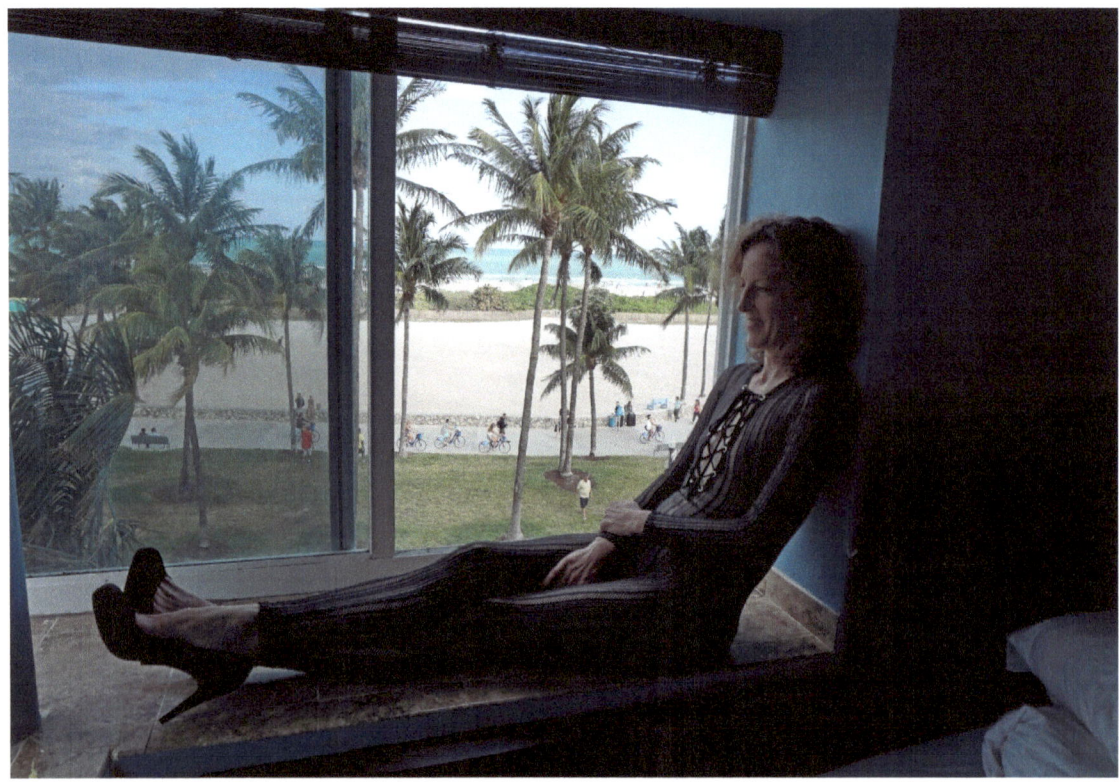

Low-impact exercise means exercise that is easy on the joints. For the sexiest people in the world, this is simply the low-impact, non-repetitive work mostly done outside in clean, fresh air also known as organic farming or at least gardening. I love gardening, but I live in cities. I try to live in the heart of the city so that I can walk as much as possible every day and use public transportation rather than drive my car.

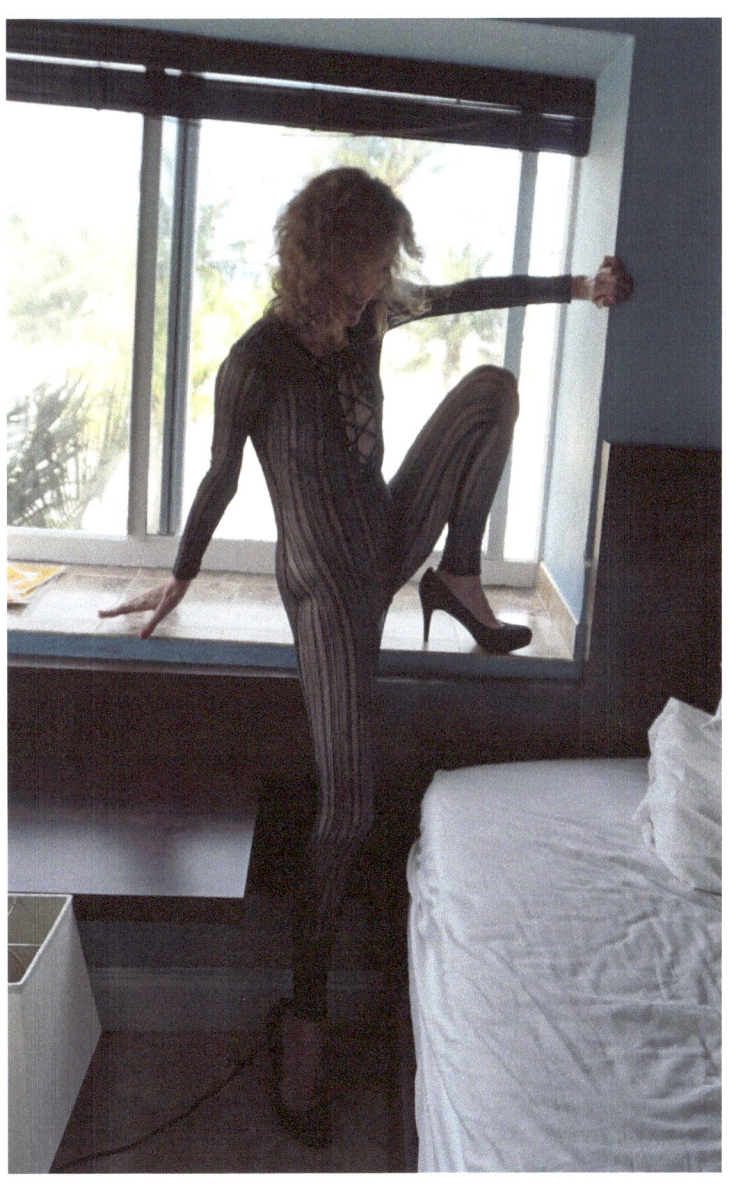

I started learning ballet at a young age and I love to dance. Not having had much opportunity to dance during the last 30 years of my life, I finally just started dancing to my favorite song at home. When any space that did exist was carpeted, I ripped out the carpet. Where there was not even enough space to dance or I couldn't rip out the carpet, I put down some towels and did yoga. Where there is a will, there is a way, trust me.

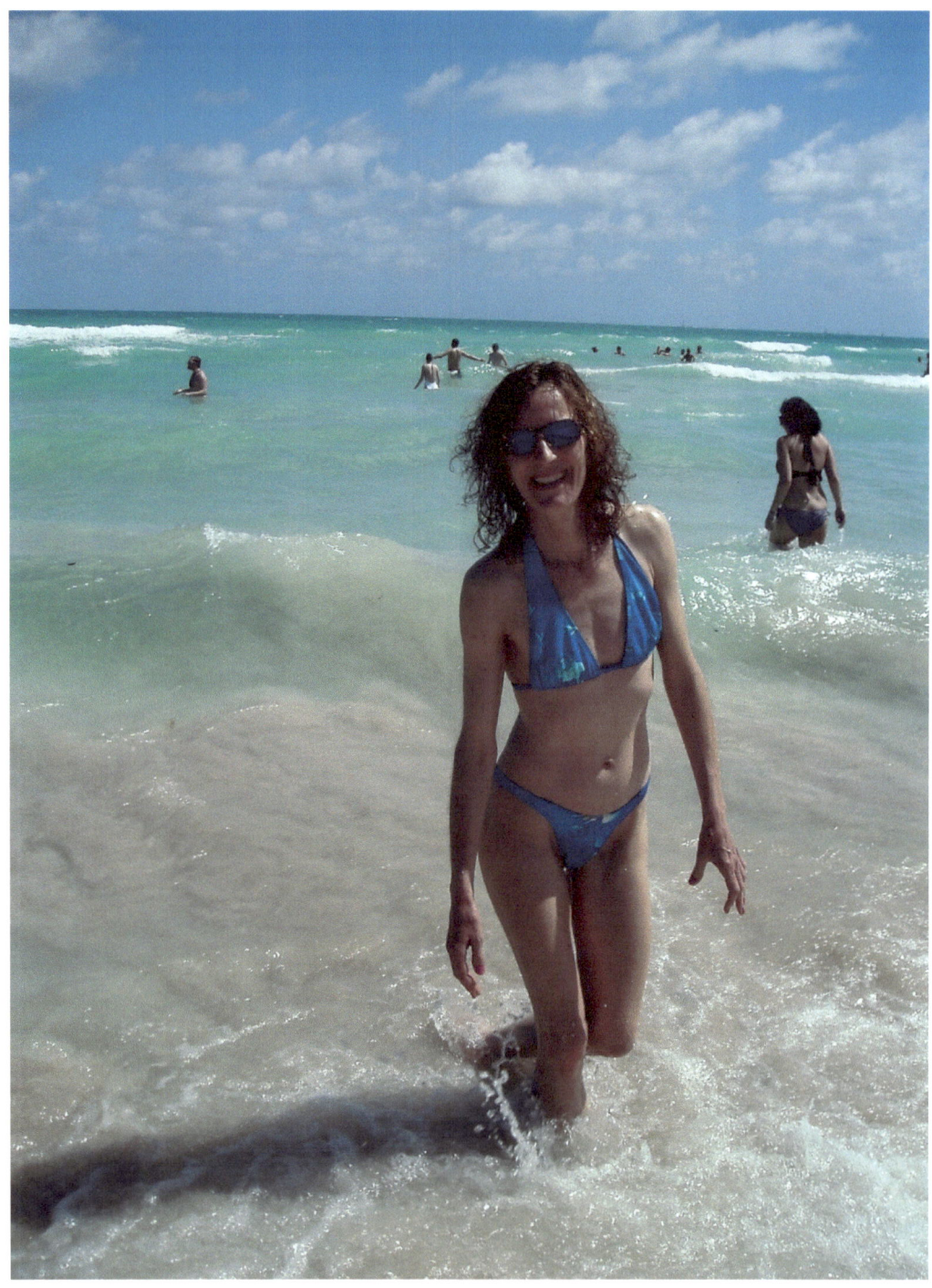

I received training in martial arts after being beat up so badly that I ended up with a concussion in grade school. Like dance, this training has stayed with me and I incorporate it into my daily exercise. I am also an avid hiker. I hiked in the alps while living and working as a scientist in Switzerland. I hiked to the tops of the highest mountains growing up in Colorado. I hiked up and down bluff tops while living in the Midwest, and I am heading back to the Grand Canyon for my next expedition in celebration of the 50th birthday of the Archangel Michael! I love being in nature and being on mountain tops because that is where I feel closest to God.

When I was 20 years old, I went to the strip club to see if I could get a job dancing there because I did not know how to support myself, especially while trying to go to college at the same time. They said I danced nice but had to go see the tit doctor. The tit doctor wanted $11,000 to implant each of my boobs with a bag of toxic liquid that later turned out to leak and make the women very sick. Why? To make my breasts look bigger because that is what men wanted to see. My tiny tits were not attractive to men, despite my ability to dance. I told that tit doctor that if I had $11,000, I wouldn't need the tits!

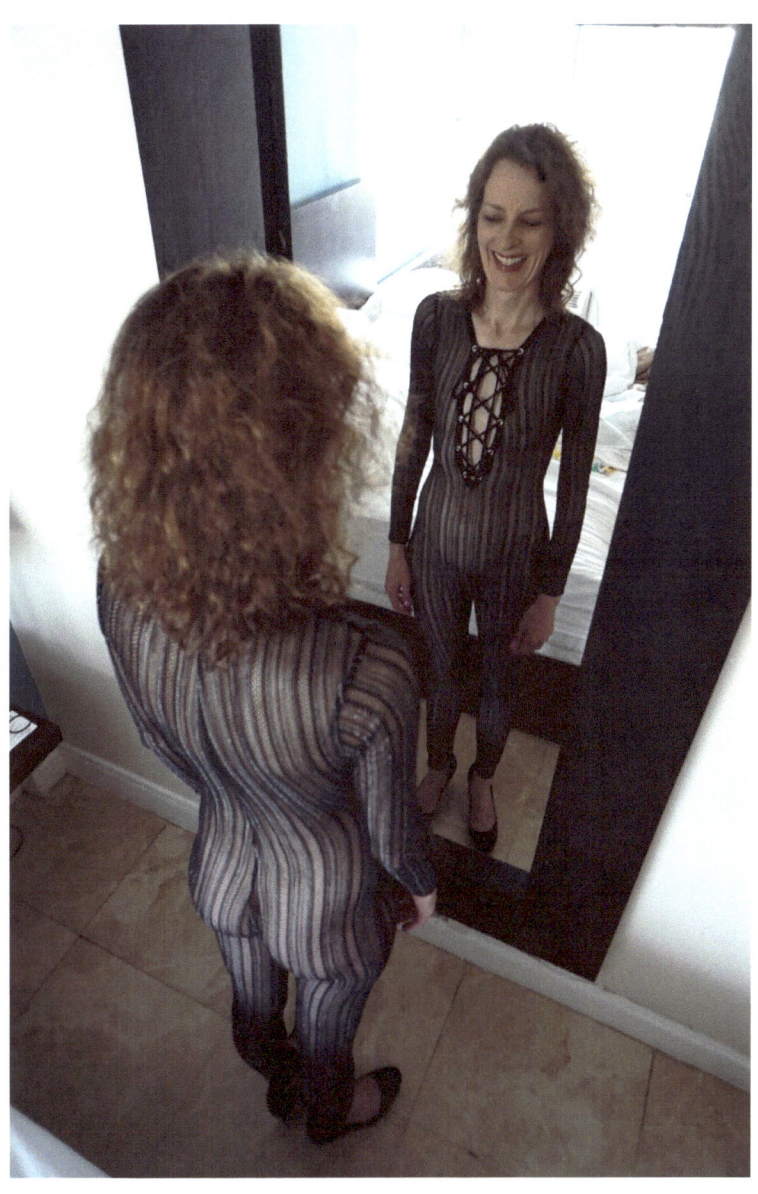

My goal is to be as naturally beautiful as possible. I have not had any plastic surgery or Botox. My teeth, hair, and nails are natural. I did not even have braces. I intend to continue aging gracefully. I use only plant-derived, natural health and beauty and cleaning products free of dyes, perfumes, fragrances and other synthetic chemicals. I use essential oils and I make my own soaps and salves.

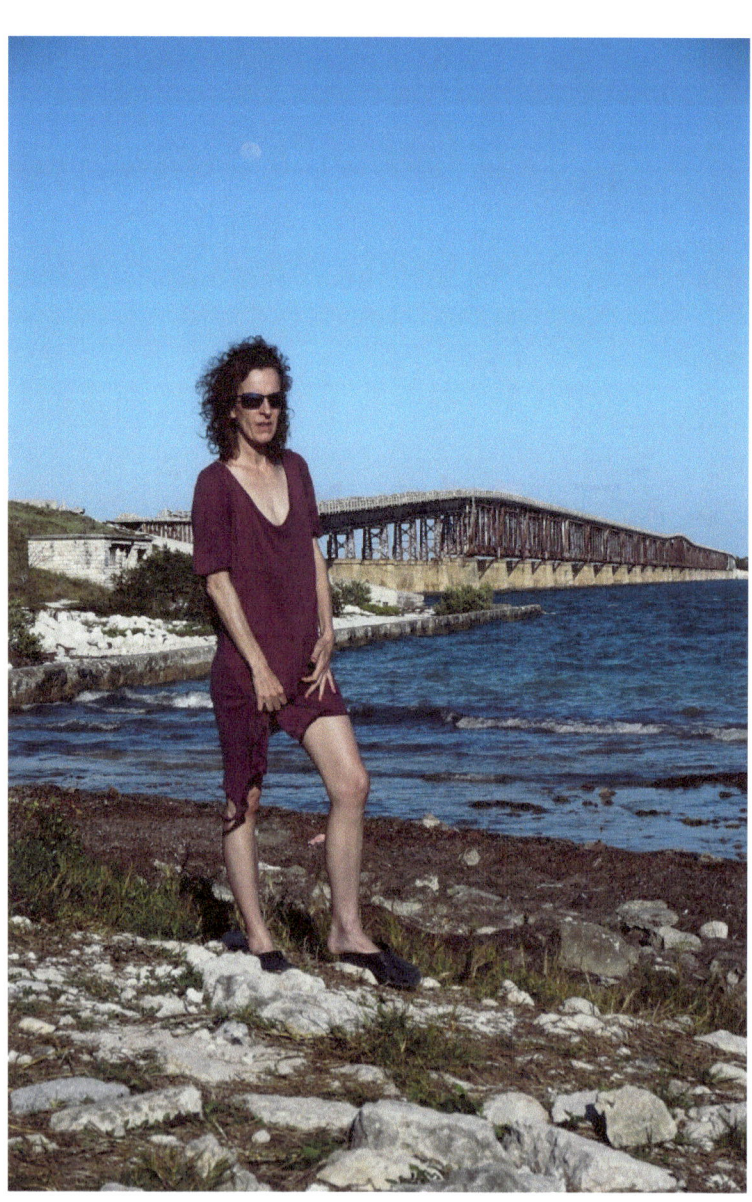

To be sexy, eat beautiful because you are what you eat. Eating beautiful means eating the most natural, whole foods you can find. So-called "organic" whole foods are farmed the old-fashioned way, the most sustainable way, without genetic engineering, brain-damaging chemicals or even fossil fuels. So-called "conventional" foods are farmed using every dirty trick in the book. That is why they are the cheapest. If there is one thing to skimp on in life, it is not food. It is not shoes either. Remember, the priorities are water, food, shelter, clothing and footwear. I try to live my life in the most practical and sustainable ways that I can. I try not to live in eccentric or selfish ways that are intended to show off and inspire envy.

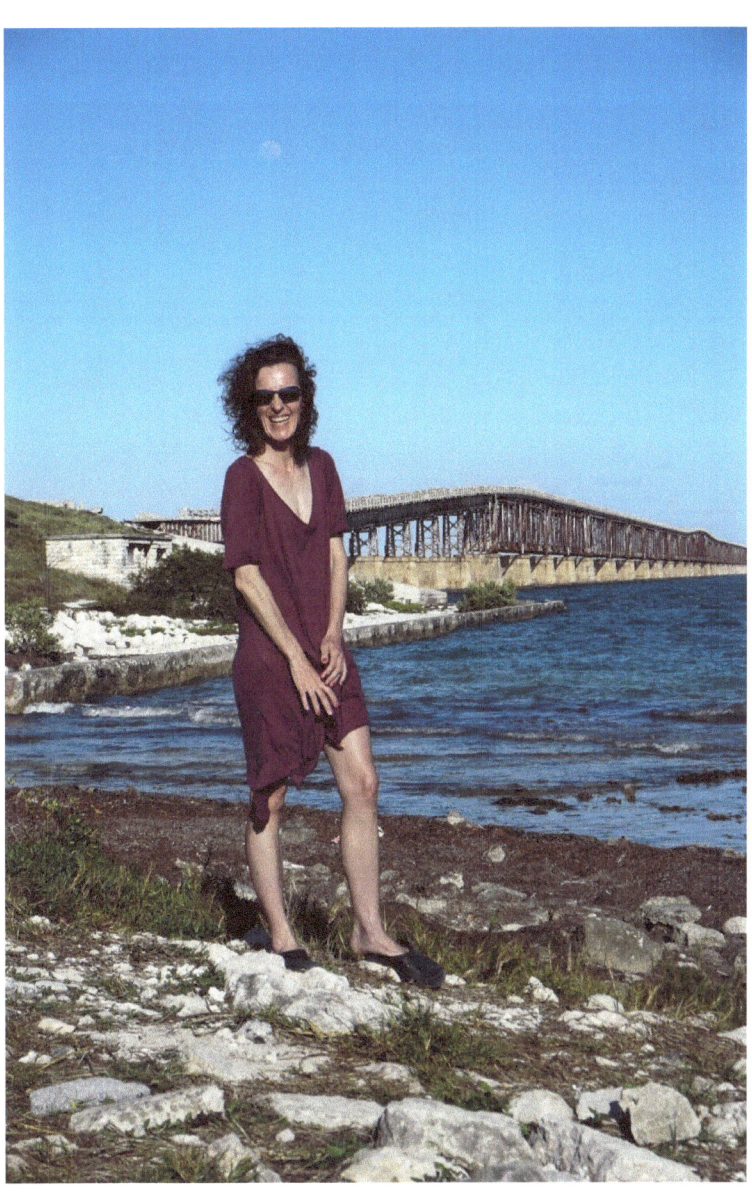

I have been gluten-free since before there was even such a term. I had to say, "I don't eat bread." This made me even more unpopular because no bread means no pizza, no cake, no pasta, no doughnuts, no sandwiches, no pastries, no hotdog or hamburger buns, no muffins, no flour tortillas, no pita bread, no cookies, no wraps nor any flour of any grain. I do not eat processed foods, preservatives, gums, monosodium glutamate or MSG (often disguised as "natural flavors" or "hydrolyzed vegetable protein" or "HVP" or "yeast extract" or "autolyzed protein"), or other chemicals. I stay away from sugar and sugary drinks. I add hot peppers, not salt, to my food. In essence, I do not eat the American diet. The American diet is not sexy.

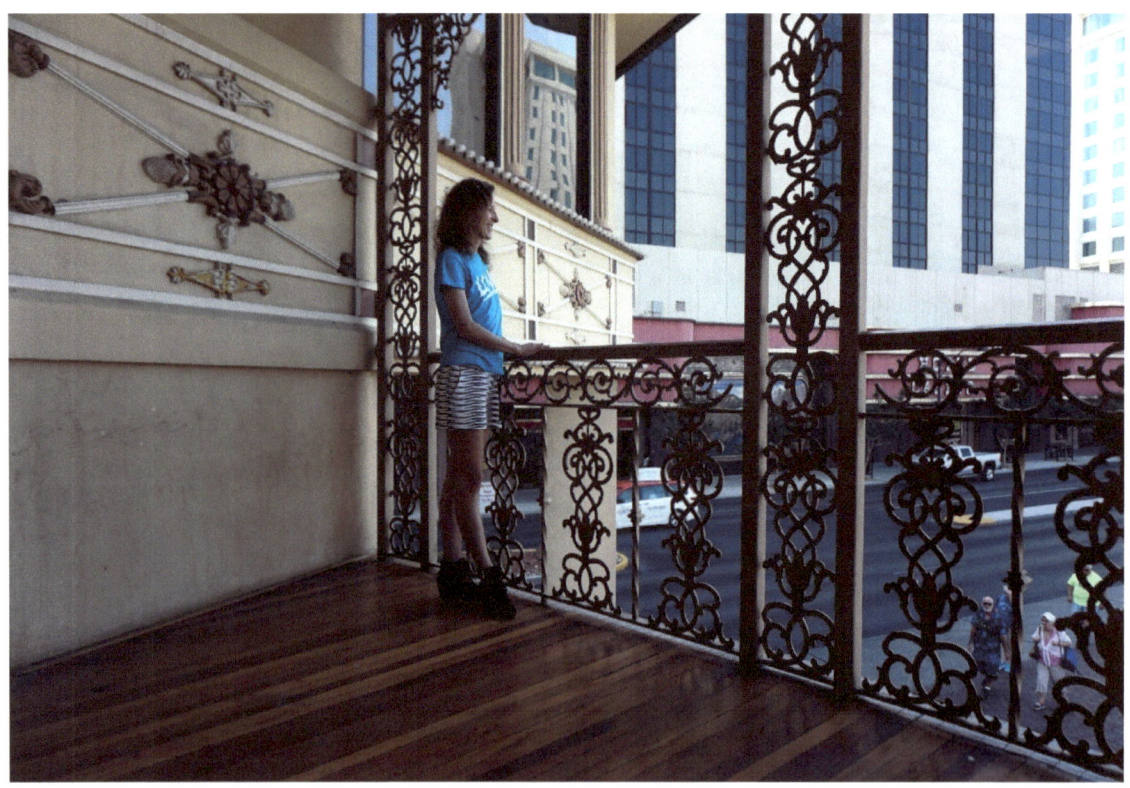

I eat whole foods such as potatoes, greens, organic free-range eggs, free-range grass-fed beef, wild-caught fish, fruits, nuts, vegetables, avocados, corn, and beans. I eat whole grains like oats, quinoa and rice. I eat organic whole milk yogurt with probiotics. I cook with olive oil. I eat hemp oil to make sure I get all the essential fatty acids we need to ingest because our bodies cannot make them. Hempseed oil has all the essential fatty acids we need, and in the most appropriate ratio as well. It smells and tastes better than fish oil, too! I drink water, mostly just water, lots of the cleanest water I can get.

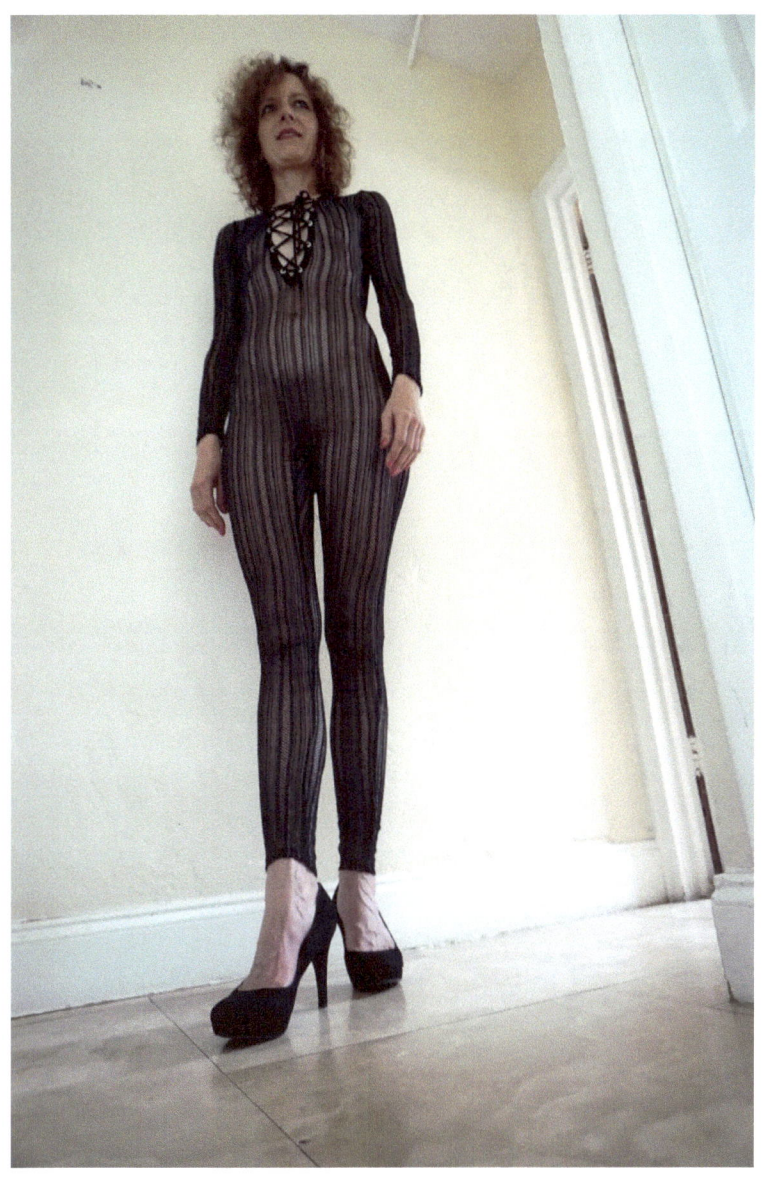

Let your medicine be your food, and let your food be your medicine, said Hippocrates, the father of medicine. My only medicine is marijuana. I do not take any prescription medications or pain killers or sleeping pills or even ibuprofen. I drink alcoholic beverages occasionally, and then only high-quality tequila and preferably mezcal. I am a medical marijuana patient because I have PTSD.

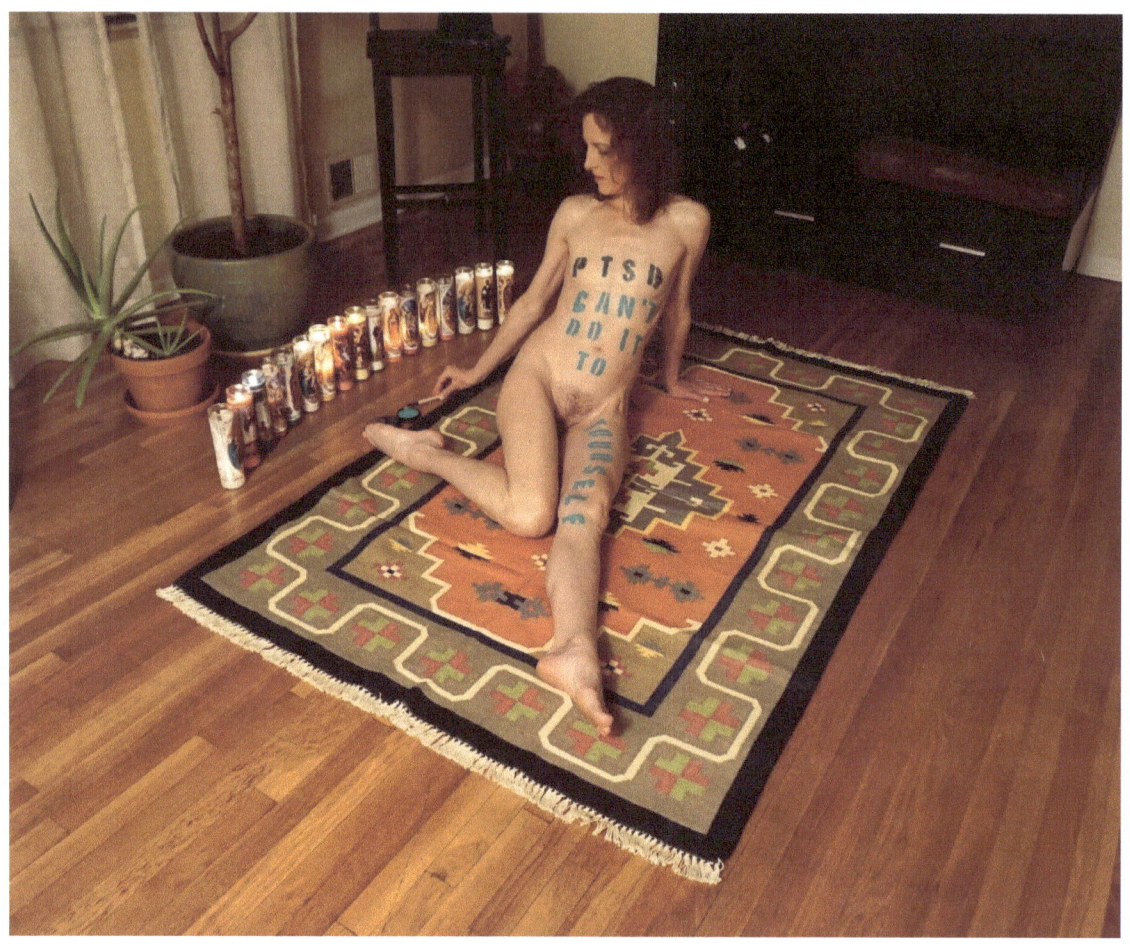

I have PTSD because my life has been a tragedy. People assume all to quickly that bad things only happen to bad people. When everyone is against you, everyone assumes you are the one who is wrong. But I am the exception. People try desperately to hold me back because I am always so far ahead. Those who stand up against oppression and injustices, and whose leadership challenges such deeply engrained and negative forces in a successful manner, can expect violent opposition. These facts of life motivate me to work even harder.

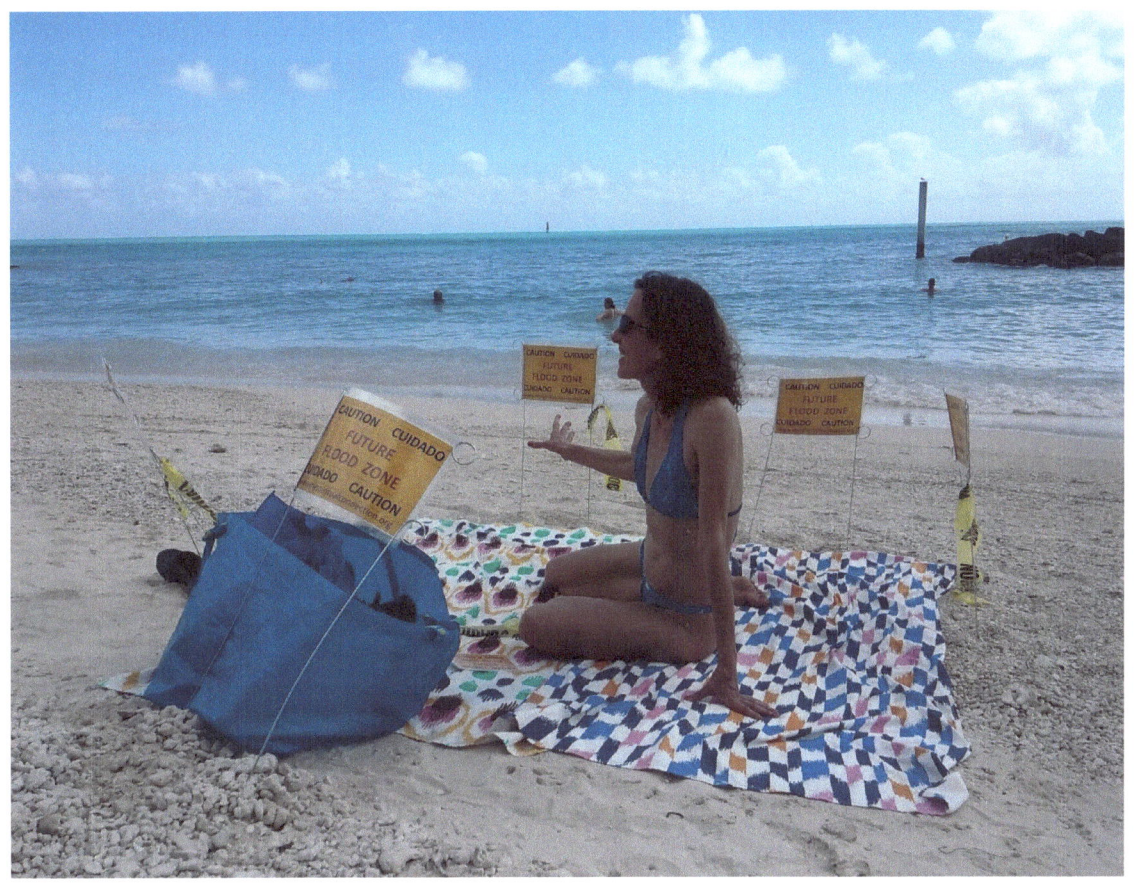

Hard work allowed me to earn my PhD degree in microbiology and immunology, but my faith and love are what keep me alive. I believe in one God. The Father, the Son, the Holy Spirit is all One. I dedicate my life to God, and I want what God wants. I listen to God before any person. God is Love and Truth. To have love and truth is to perform non-merit-seeking acts of charity (to love thy neighbor as thyself), to believe the truths of faith, and to live according to the 10 Commandments, which are to do no evil.

It is never too late to be your highest self.

Love,

Marie

I leave you with a summary of the 10 most important things to do to be sexy:

#10: Rest

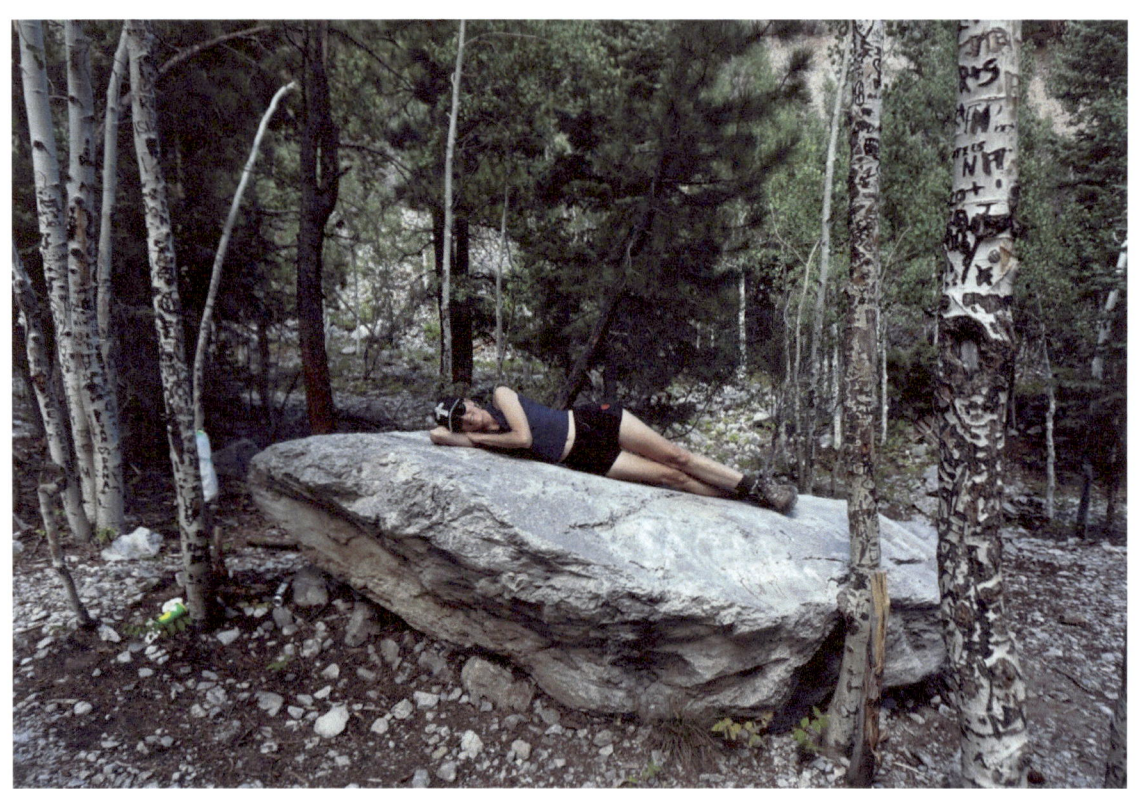

#9: De-stress

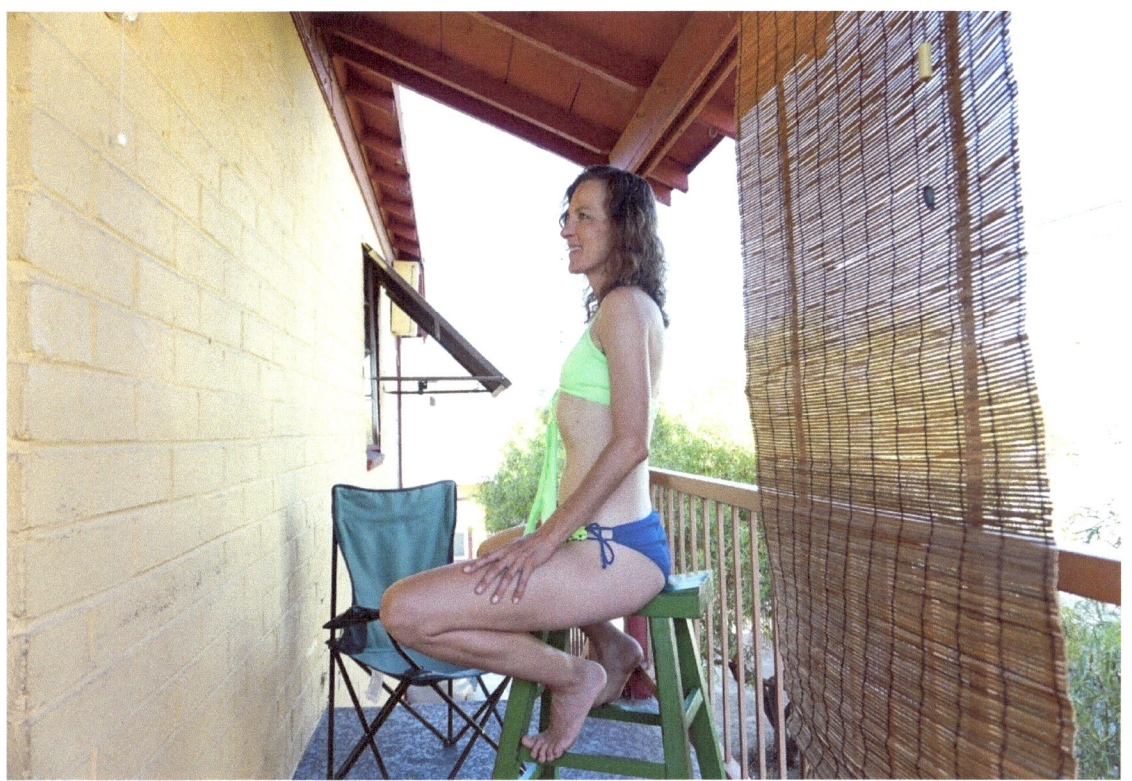

#8: Be yourself

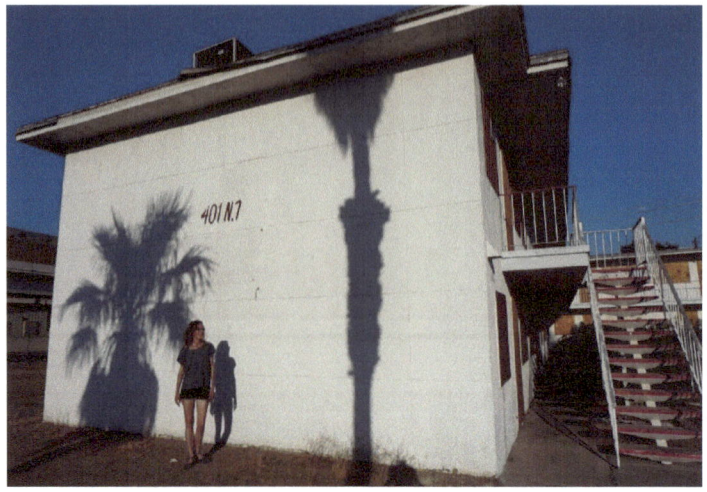

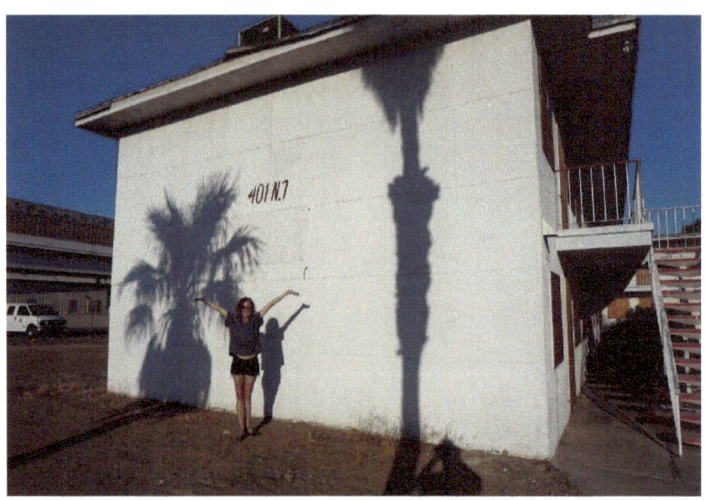

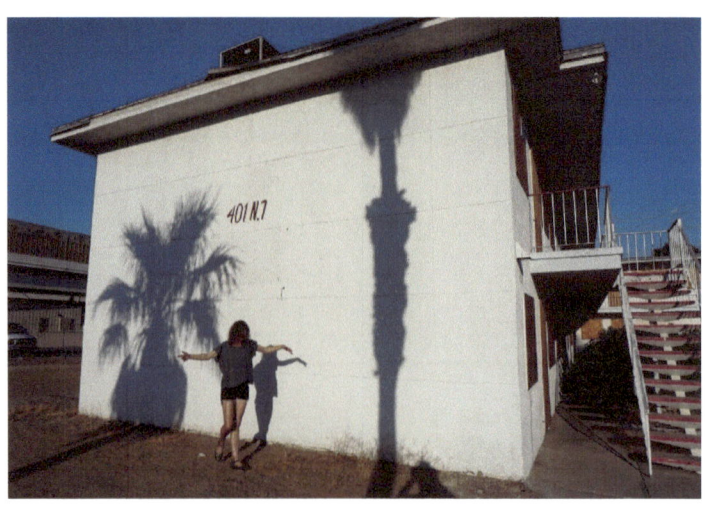

#7: Be natural

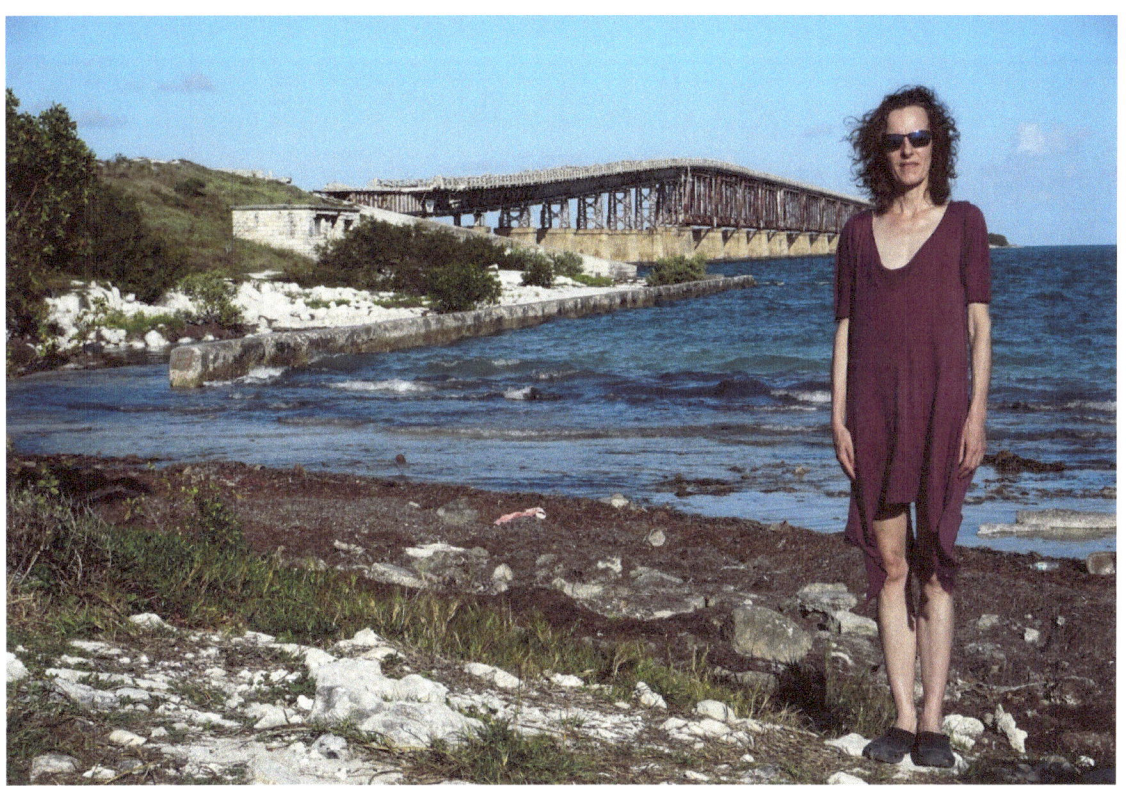

#6: Exercise

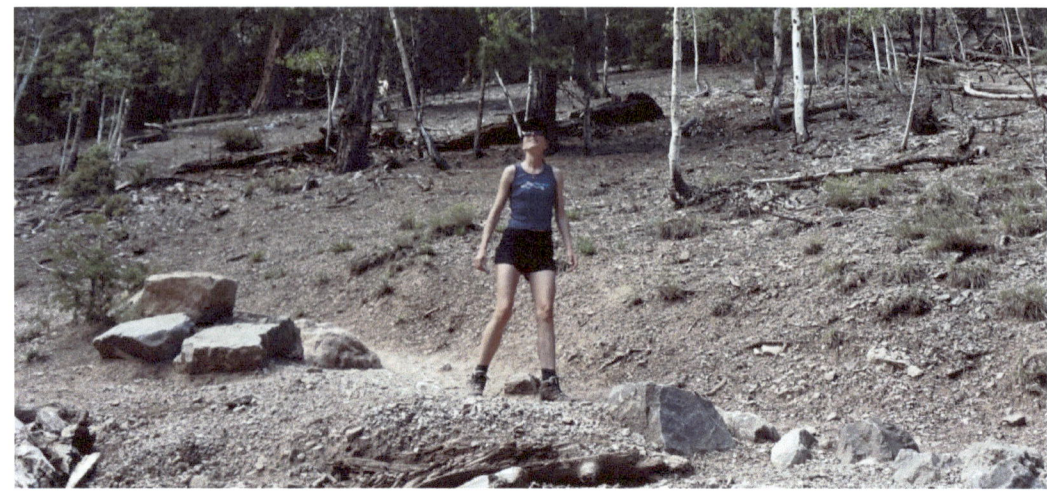

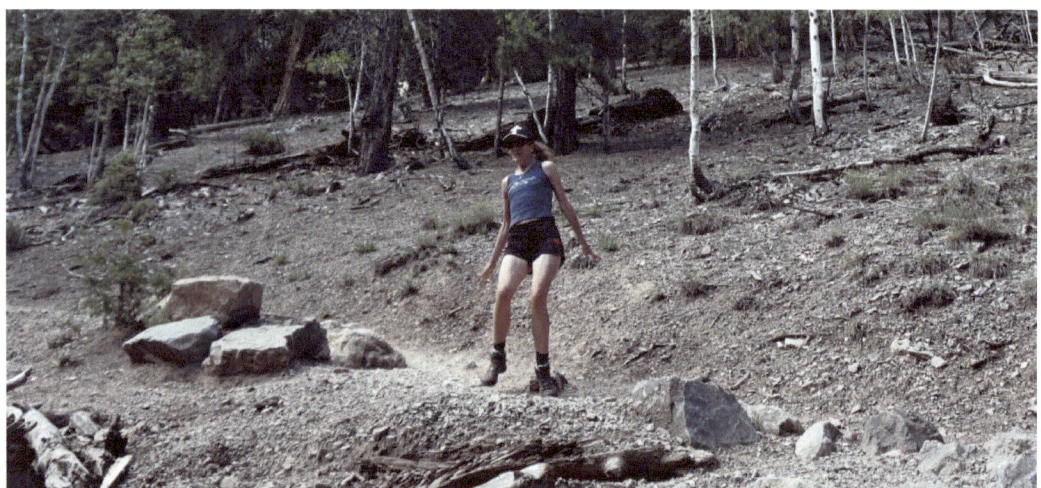

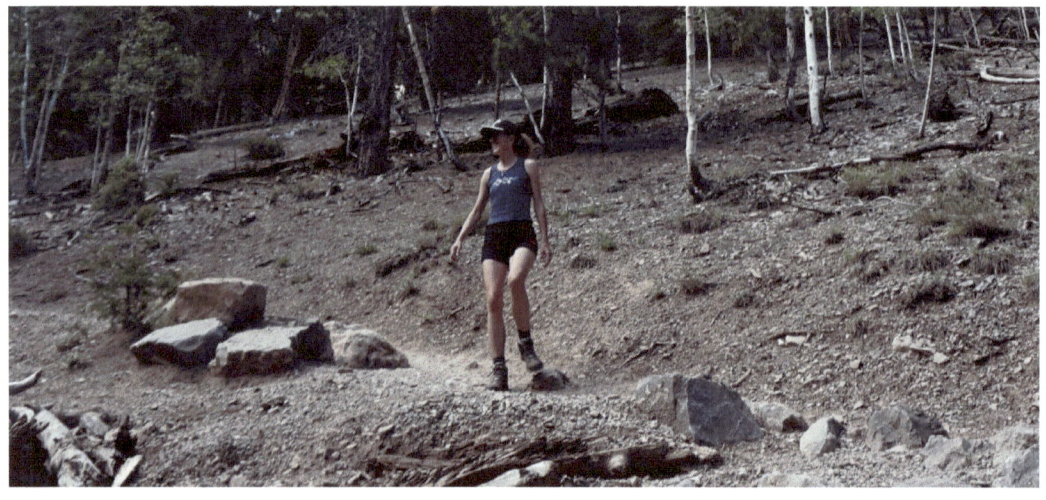

#5: Eat sexy

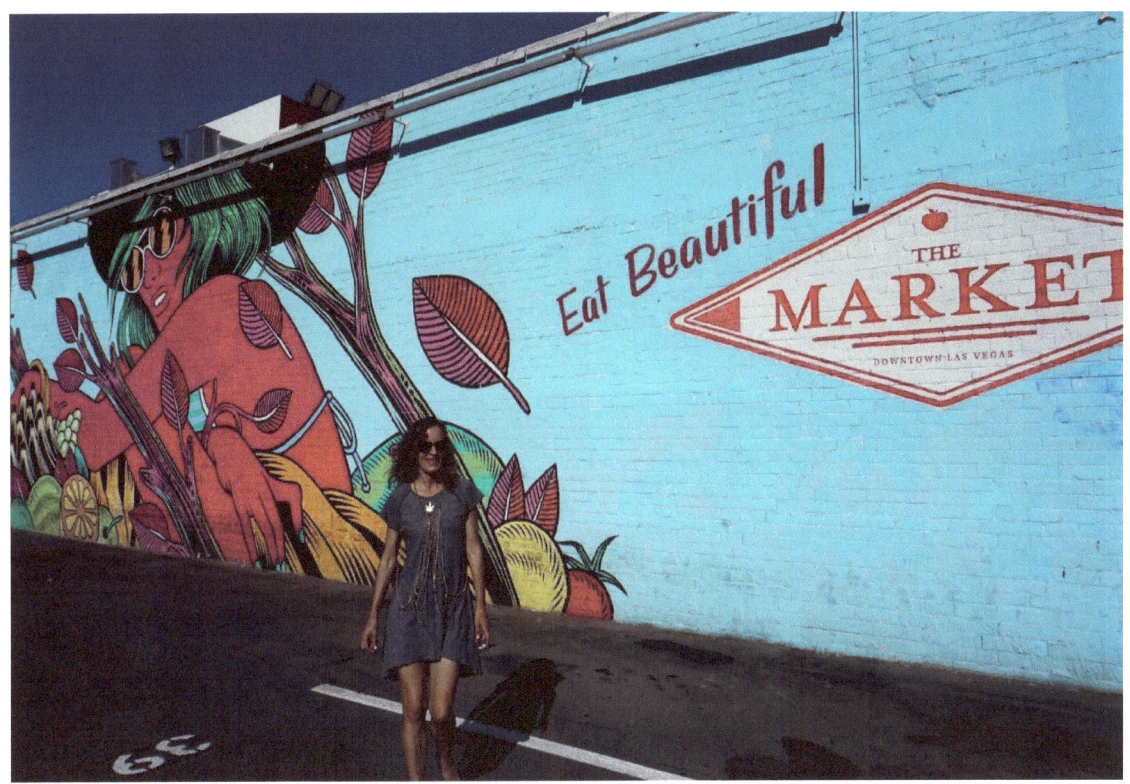

#4: Live in accordance with the 10 Commandments

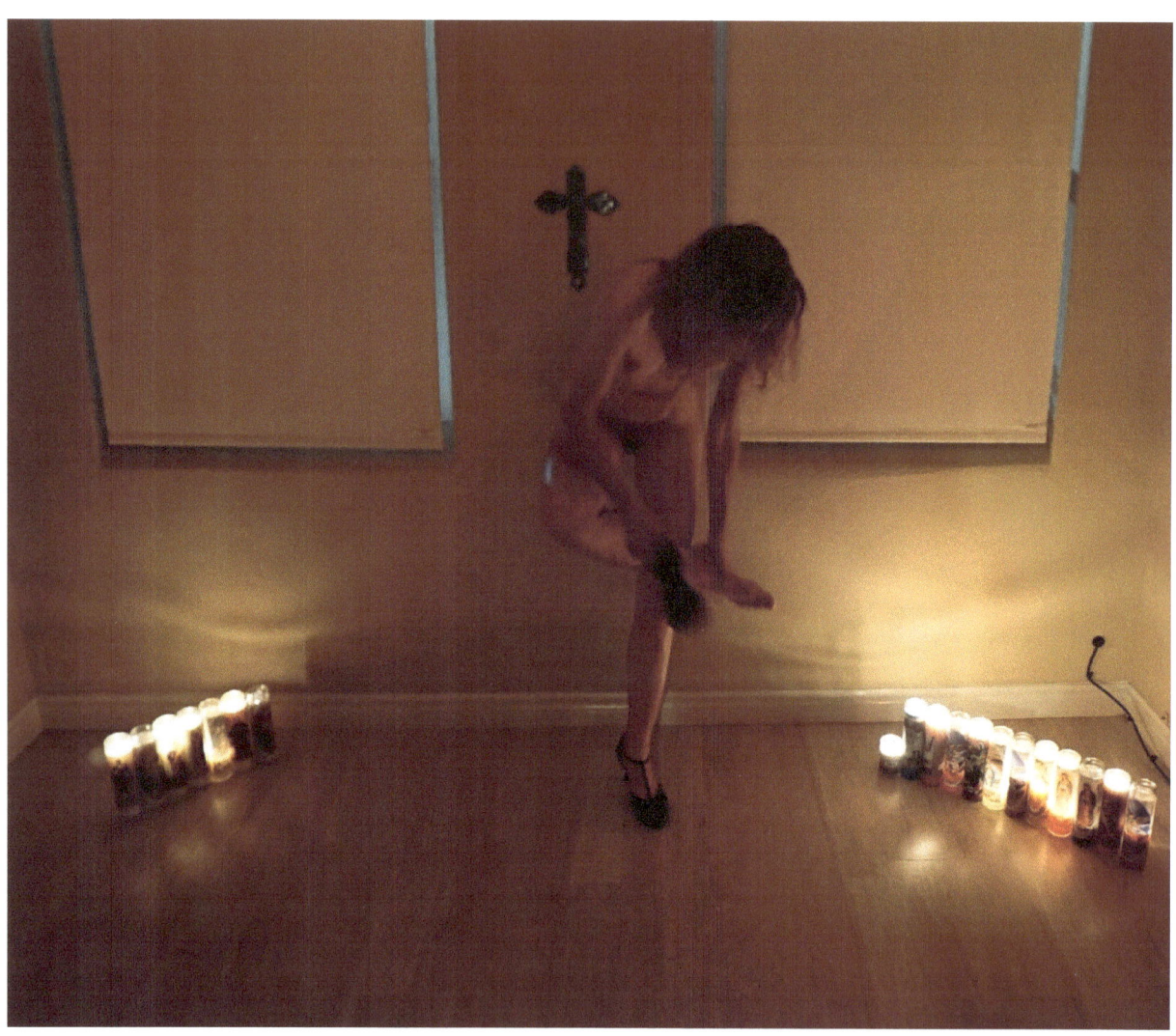

#3: Believe the truths of faith; be optimistic; be positive

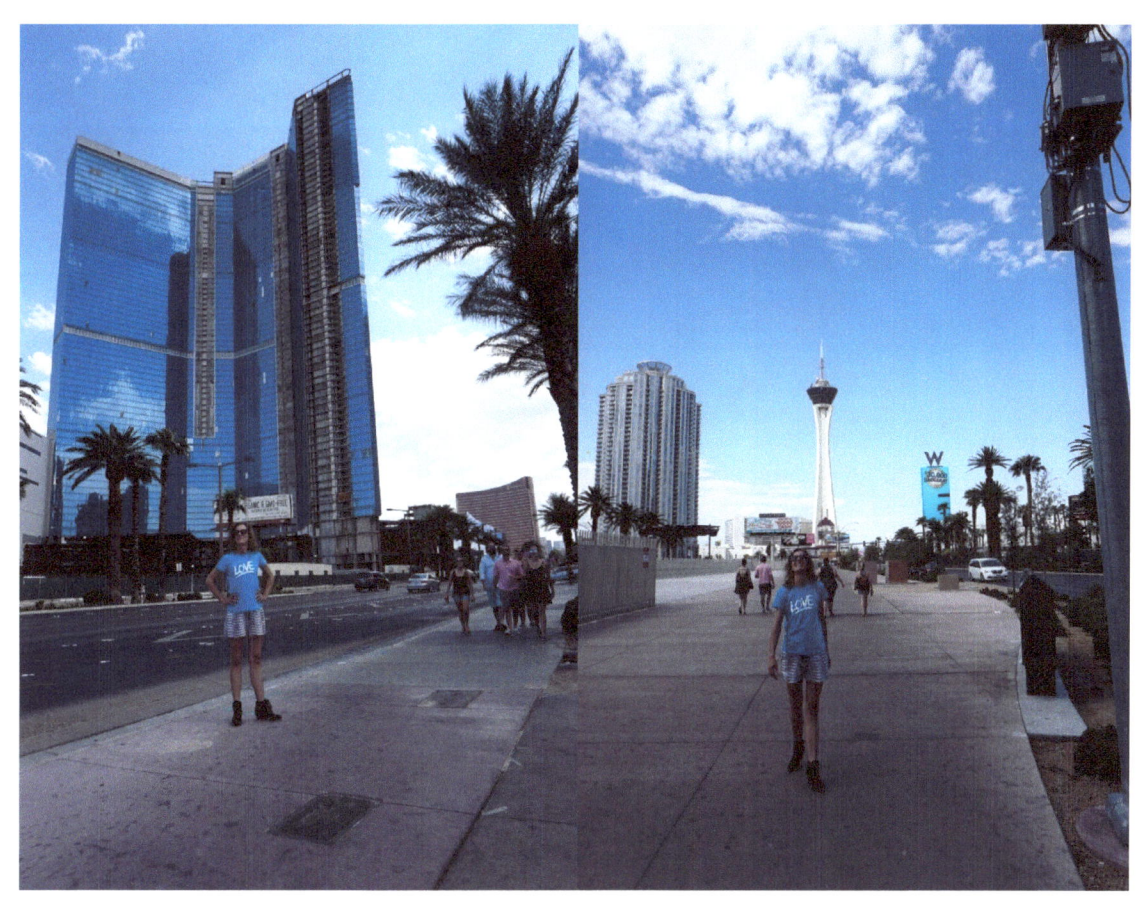

#2: Do good, charitable deeds (love thy neighbor as thyself) without needing or even wanting to be rewarded or acknowledged

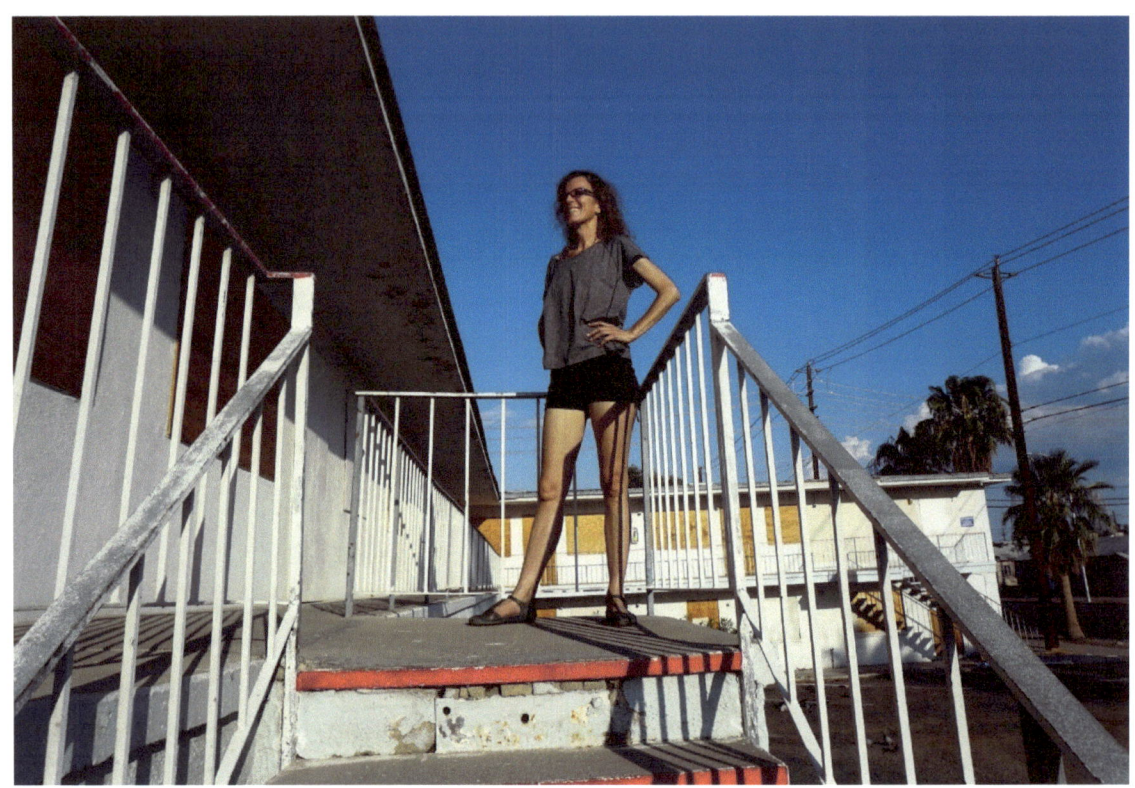

If I could, I would fix up this place so that homeless people could live here in a sustainable manner. I would foster positive interactions between homeless people and more fortunate individuals with open minds and open hearts. I would create affordable and healthy housing as well as affordable opportunities to engage in social dancing with inspirational music. Everyone deserves to live in a place that is not over-crowded and that has a window on at least two sides so that fresh air can flow through.

#1: Believe in one God

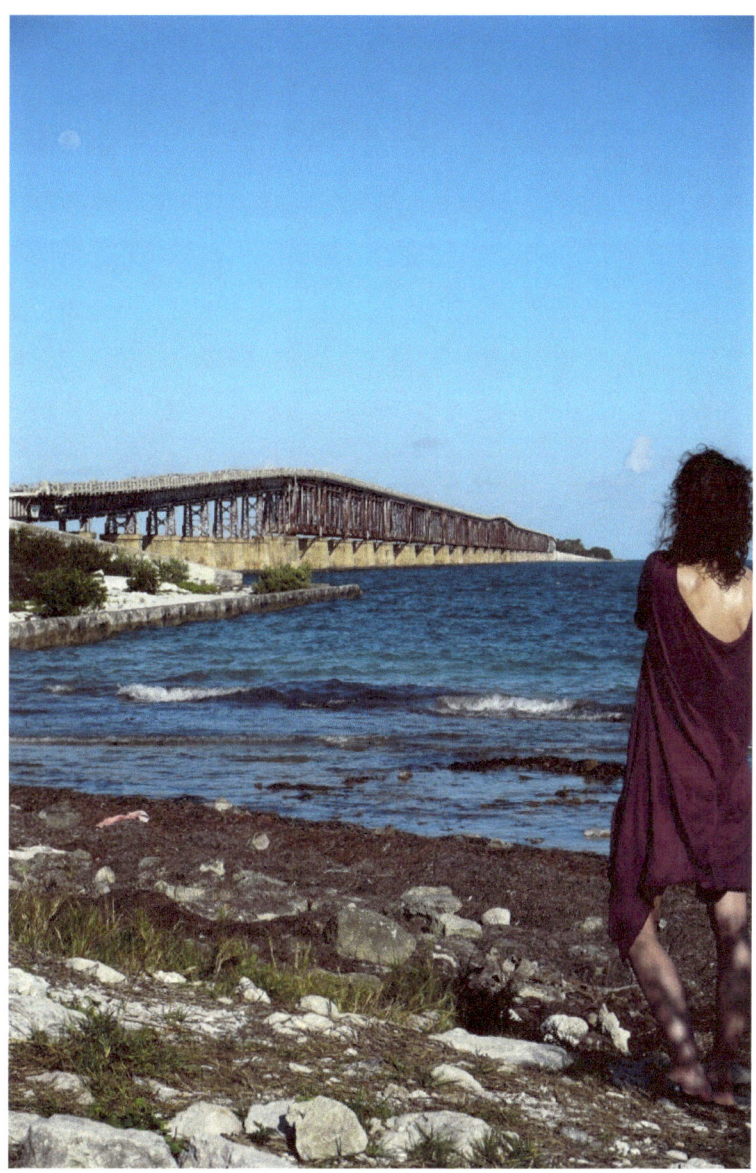

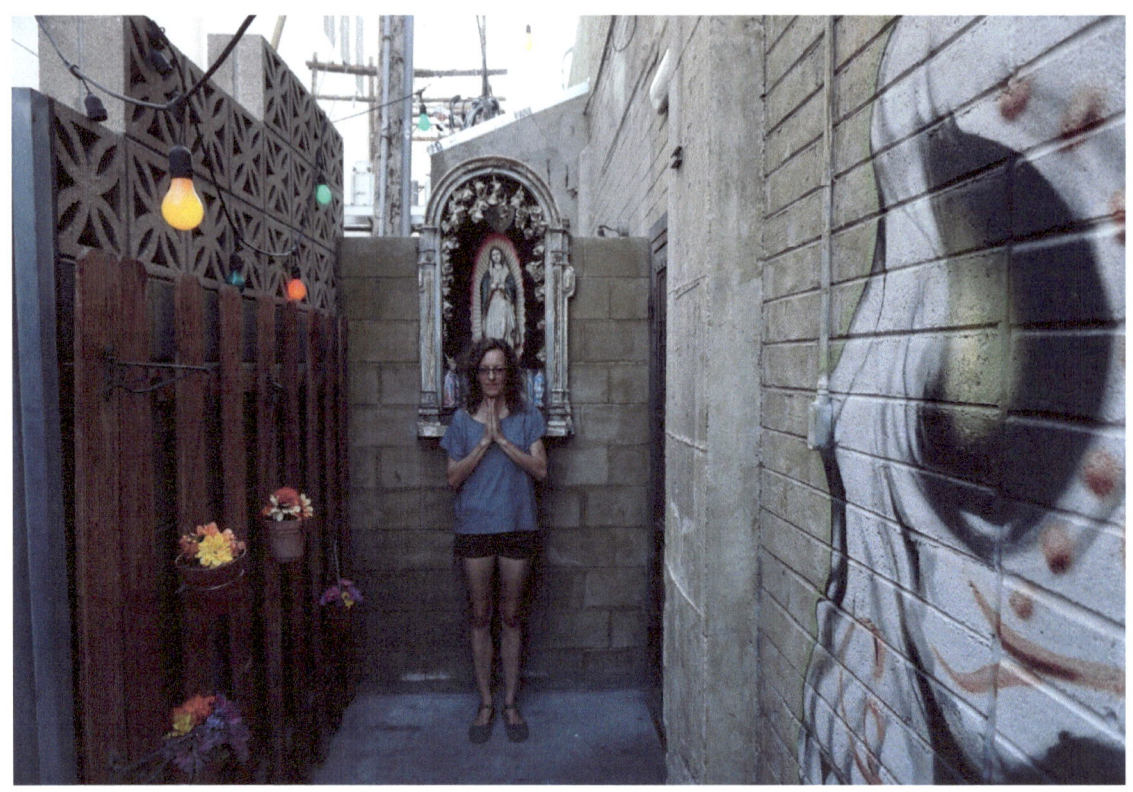

About the author, model, and photographer:

Marie D. Kube, Ph.D., is an award-winning scientist-writer who advocates every way she can for an end to social injustices stemming from control by evil forces of our necessities: water, food, shelter, clothing and footwear. She blogs on two websites, www.myspiritualconnection.org and www.myspiritualassociation.com, featuring *Instructions for Helping to Improve the Human Condition*.

About the photographer and editor:

Michael G. Klug, Ph.D., is a professor of life sciences who empowers people through education, particularly under-represented populations. In his spare time, he dedicates his talents to supporting art and artists by serving as a photographer and editor.

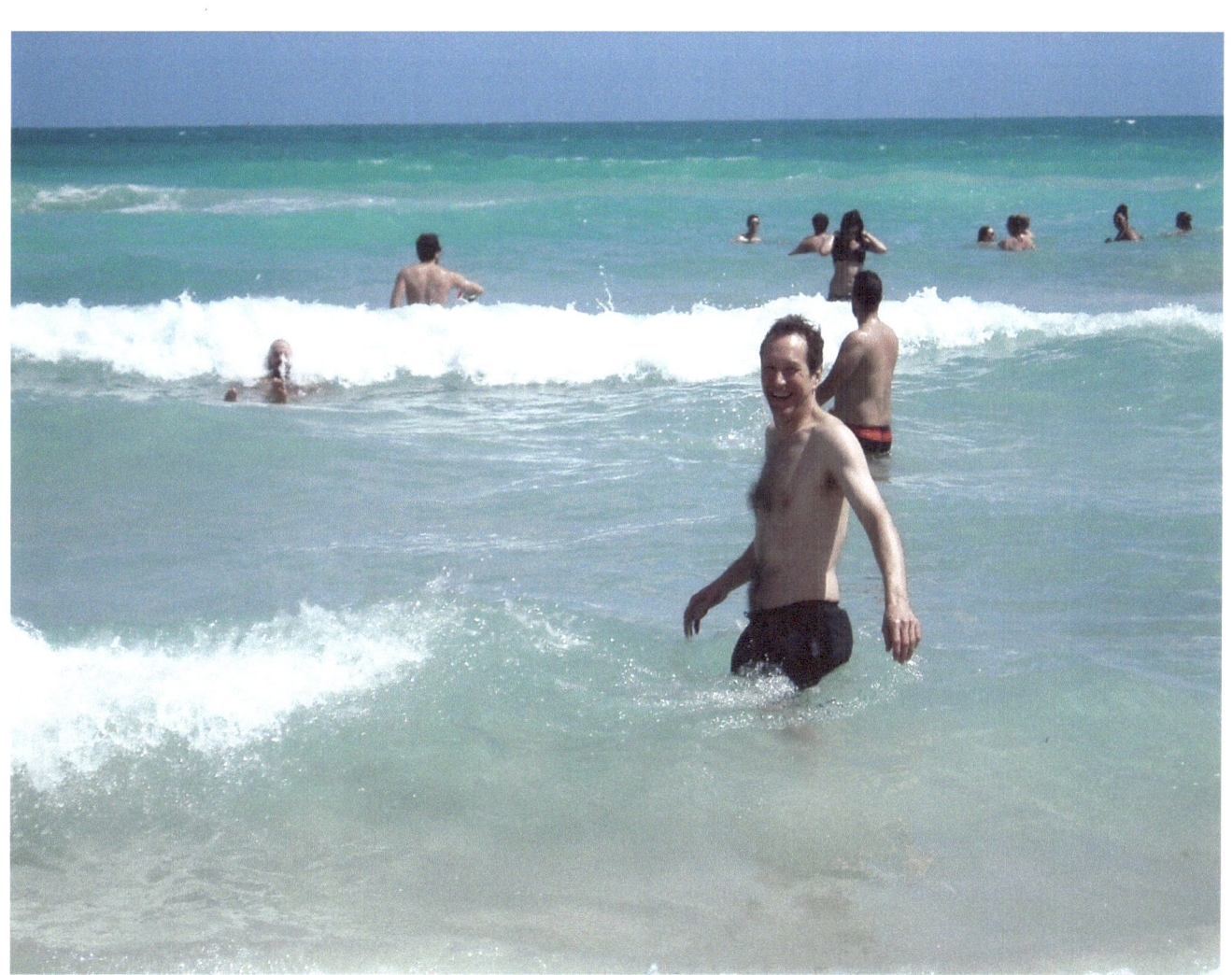

www.ingramcontent.com/pod-product-compliance
Lightning Source LLC
Chambersburg PA
CBHW040057250526
45473CB00043B/1812